FOCUS

on Grammar and Punctuation

Grammar and Punctuation

Book 1

Louis Fidge

Collins

Using this book

This book will help you to understand grammar and punctuation, and improve your writing. You will learn how sentences are structured and formed, how words work together and the rules of our language. Punctuation goes hand in hand with grammar – punctuation marks make writing easier to understand.

What's in a unit

Each unit is set out in the same way as the example here. There are also Progress Units to help you check how well you are doing.

Unit heading
This tells you what you will be learning about

The rule
This explains the rule and gives an example

Making sure
Activities to practise and develop your understanding

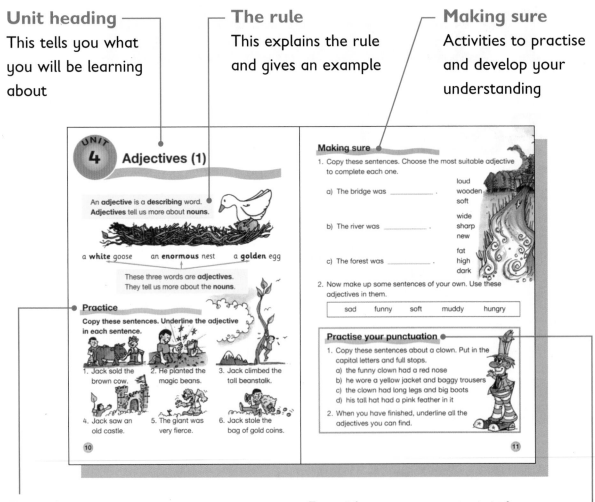

Practice
Activities to practise and check your understanding

Practise your punctuation
Activities to practise and check your punctuation

Contents

Writing Sentences

A **sentence** is a group of words that **makes sense** on its own.
A **sentence** starts with a **capital letter**.
Most **sentences** end with a **full stop**.

The caterpillar is eating a leaf.

This **is** a **sentence**.
It makes **sense**.

wiggling up and down

This **is not** a **sentence**.
It **does not make sense** on its own.

Practice

Which of these are sentences?
Copy the sentences into your book.

1. Most caterpillars are green.
2. A spider has eight legs.
3. in the night
4. Snails live in shells.
5. is very sunny
6. A fly has wings.
7. like a star
8. Worms live under the ground.

Making sure

Match the beginnings and endings of these sentences.
Write the sentences in your book. The first one has been
done for you.

1. A bird   look like flying mice.
2. Frogs   has prickles.
3. A hedgehog   flies in the sky.
4. Bats   moves very slowly.
5. A tortoise   change into butterflies.
6. Caterpillars   live in ponds.

A bird flies in the sky.

Practise your punctuation

Arrange these words so that they make sentences.
Remember the full stops and capital letters.

1. sting wasps
2. are busy ants always
3. grow frogs tadpoles into
4. a tail mouse a long has
5. noise bees a buzzing make
6. their spiders catch in webs insects

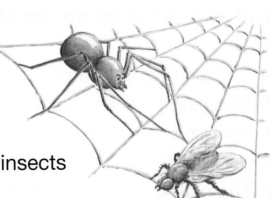

Verbs (1)

A **verb** is a word that describes actions.
A **verb** tells us what someone is **doing**
or what is **happening**.

The farmer **drives** his tractor.

This is a **verb**. It tells us what the farmer is **doing**.

Practice

Copy these sentences. Underline the verb in each
sentence. The first one has been done for you.

1. The girl <u>dug</u> the garden.
2. She planted some seeds.
3. The girl watered the seeds.
4. The seeds grew into lovely flowers.
5. The girl picked the flowers.
6. She gave the flowers to her Gran.

Making sure

Choose a verb from the box to complete each sentence.

sells	climbs	works	mends	types	flies

1. A farmer _____ on a farm.
2. A pilot _____ aeroplanes.
3. A baker _____ bread and cakes.
4. A secretary _____ letters.
5. A mountaineer _____ mountains.
6. A plumber _____ burst pipes.

Practise your punctuation

1. Copy these sentences.
   Remember to put in the capital letters and full stops.
   a) one day a farmer was digging his field
   b) it was hot work
   c) suddenly his spade hit something hard
   d) the farmer dug faster
   e) he found a small wooden box
   f) the farmer opened the box

2. Now write a sentence about what
   the farmer found in the box.

UNIT 3 Nouns (1)

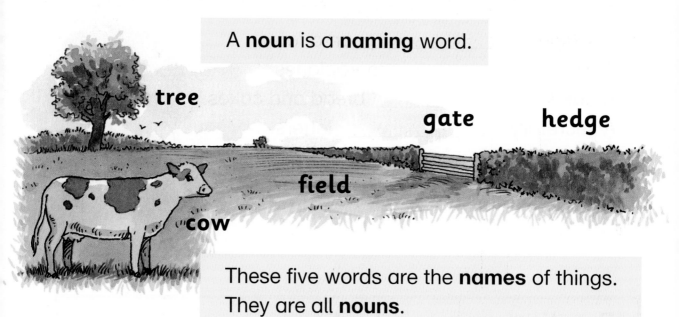

A **noun** is a **naming** word.

tree

gate   hedge

field

cow

These five words are the **names** of things.
They are all **nouns**.

Practice

All these things come from cows.

milk   cheese   butter   cream   ice cream

Copy and complete these sentences using the nouns above.

1. I spread _____ on my bread.
2. _____ is very cold.
3. I like to drink a glass of _____ .
4. Strawberries and _____ are lovely.
5. You can put _____ in a sandwich.

Making sure

1. Copy these sentences. There are two nouns in each sentence. Underline each noun.
   a) Hens lay eggs.
   b) Wool comes from sheep.
   c) The horse ran out of the stable.
   d) The cat chased a mouse.

2. Now draw a chart like this in your book.
   Write the names of five different animals in each column.

Animals you can keep as pets	Farm animals	Wild animals

Practise your punctuation

1. Which verb goes with each noun?
   The first one has been done for you.

Nouns		Verbs	
cows	dogs	bray	moo
cats	birds	bleat	neigh
mice	sheep	sing	mew
horses	donkeys	squeak	bark

Cows moo.

2. Check that you have put a capital letter and a full stop in each sentence.

Adjectives (1)

An **adjective** is a **describing** word.
Adjectives tell us more about **nouns**.

a **white** goose   an **enormous** nest   a **golden** egg

These three words are **adjectives**.
They tell us more about the **nouns**.

Practice

Copy these sentences. Underline the adjective in each sentence.

1. Jack sold the brown cow.

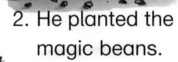

2. He planted the magic beans.

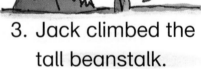

3. Jack climbed the tall beanstalk.

4. Jack saw an old castle.

5. The giant was very fierce.

6. Jack stole the bag of gold coins.

Making sure

1. Copy these sentences. Choose the most suitable adjective to complete each one.

loud
wooden
soft

a) The bridge was _____ .

wide
sharp
new

b) The river was _____ .

fat
high
dark

c) The forest was _____ .

2. Now make up some sentences of your own. Use these adjectives in them.

sad	funny	soft	muddy	hungry

Practise your punctuation

1. Copy these sentences about a clown. Put in the capital letters and full stops.
   a) the funny clown had a red nose
   b) he wore a yellow jacket and baggy trousers
   c) the clown had long legs and big boots
   d) his tall hat had a pink feather in it

2. When you have finished, underline all the adjectives you can find.

Questions

A **question** is a **sentence** that we use **when we want to know something**.

Whenever we write a **sentence** that is a **question** we must:

- put a **capital letter** at the beginning .
- put a **question mark** at the end.

What is your name**?**

Which planet are you from**?**

Practice

These questions and answers have got mixed up. Write them in your book. Match each question with its answer. The first one has been done for you.

Questions	*Answers*
1. What colour is grass?	It is in March.
2. Do you have a pet?	It is my birthday.
3. When is your birthday?	I have a cat.
4. Where is my book?	It is green.
5. Why are you so happy?	You left it in the bedroom.

What colour is grass? It is green.

Making sure

Write the question you think each of these people is asking. The first one has been done for you.

1.

What is the time?

2.

3.

4.

Practise your punctuation

Copy this rhyme.
Put in capital letters, full stops and question marks where they are needed.

what is pink
i think a rose is pink
what is red
the hat on my head is red
what is green
grass is green with flowers in between
what is orange
a lemon is yellow but an orange is orange

a or an?

We use **an** in front of a word that begins with a **vowel**.
There are **five vowels**:
a e i o u

We use **a** in front of a word that begins with a **consonant**.
All letters that are **not vowels** are called **consonants**.

an apple   **a** banana

Try changing the **a** and the **an** around.
          a apple   **an** banana
Do the words **sound** right?

Practice

Write a or an before each of these nouns.

1. _____ pencil

2. _____ cake

3. _____ egg

4. _____ octopus

5. _____ ant

6. _____ snake

Making sure

1. Write **a** or **an** in front of each of these adjectives. Think of a noun to go with each adjective. The first one has been done for you.

a) _an_ exciting _adventure_   b) ____ hot _____

c) ____ old _____   d) ____ long _____

e) ____ clever _____   f) ____ interesting _____

g) ____ pretty _____   h) ____ amazing _____

2. Now make up a sentence containing each of your answers.

Practise your punctuation

1. The answers to these riddles have got mixed up. Write the riddles and answers correctly. Remember the capital letters, full stops and question marks.

a) *Riddle* :   Where does a baby ape sleep?
   Answer :   A towel gets wet as it dries.

b) *Riddle* :   What has hands and a face but no legs?
   Answer :   A baby ape sleeps in an apricot.

c) *Riddle* :   What gets wet as it dries?
   Answer :   A clock has hands and a face but no legs.

2. Underline **a** or **an** in each riddle.
   Check that you have used them correctly.

Verbs (2)

What is Sam doing? Sam **is singing**.

Sometimes verbs can be made up of more than one word.

Practice

What are the children doing?
Write the correct verbs in your book.

shouting	sleeping	sitting	playing	singing
drinking	eating	writing	painting	dancing
hiding	skipping	jumping	laughing	reading

Making sure

Copy these sentences. Choose one of the verbs in the box to complete each sentence.

eating	reading	watching	barking
	drinking	delivering	looking

1. Tom is _____ television.
2. Sam is _____ out of the window.
3. The baby is _____ her dinner.
4. The postman is _____ some letters.
5. The dog is _____ at the postman.
6. Mrs Green is _____ a newspaper.
7. The cat is _____ a bowl of milk.

Practise your punctuation

1. These are not sentences. They do not make sense.
   Every sentence must have a verb in it.
   Think of some suitable verbs, and then write the
   sentences. The first one has been done for you.
   a) the footballer the ball The footballer <u>kicked</u> the ball.
   b) the baker some bread
   c) a boy over the wall
   d) a pilot an aeroplane
   e) the girl her bike

2. Check that you have used capital letters
   and full stops correctly.

3. Underline the verb in each of your sentences.

Nouns (2)

Remember – a **noun** is a **naming** word.

teacher   **school**   **lunchbox**

A **noun** is the **name** of a **person**, **place** or **thing**.

Practice

1. Complete each sentence with the name of the place where the animal lives. The first one has been done for you.

stable	sty	shell	nest
den	burrow	web	hive

a) An ant lives in a __nest__.   b) A rabbit lives in a _____.

c) A bee lives in a _____.   d) A horse lives in a _____.

e) A snail lives in a _____.   f) A spider lives in a _____.

g) A lion lives in a _____.   h) A pig lives in a _____.

2. Now underline the two nouns in each sentence.

Making sure

Underline the odd one out. Explain your answer.
The first one has been done for you.

1. horse sheep <u>bus</u> cow
   Bus is the odd one out. The others are all names of animals.

2. apple shoe boot trainer

3. potato bicycle carrot cabbage

4. guitar trumpet piano computer

5. knife fork plate spoon

6. teacher dentist doctor rabbit

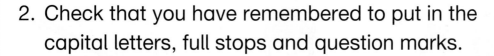

Practise your punctuation

1. Make up a question to go with each answer.
   The first one has been done for you.
   a) *Question* : What does a cow eat?
      Answer :   It eats grass.
   b) *Question* :
      Answer :   It is yellow.
   c) *Question* :
      Answer :   It is an insect.

2. Check that you have remembered to put in the
   capital letters, full stops and question marks.

3. Underline all the nouns in your questions and answers.

UNIT 9

Adjectives (2)

Remember – an **adjective** is a **describing** word.

a **happy** girl

a **frightened** girl

a **grumpy** girl

These **adjectives describe** the girl.
They tell us more about her.

Practice

Copy these descriptions. Underline the adjective in each one. The first one has been done for you.

1. the <u>tall</u> giant

2. shiny apples

3. an open door

4. a glass slipper

5. a long nose

6. fierce dragons

7. a rich king

8. an angry elf

9. a sharp needle

Making sure

1. Choose suitable adjectives from the box to complete this description of a cat. The first one has been done for you.

bright	sharp	soft	big
long	green	black	pointed

a) Patch was a ___big___ ___black___ cat.

b) He had _____ fur and a _____ tail.

c) His eyes were _____ and _____ .

d) His ears were _____ .

e) Patch had _____ claws on his paws.

2. Write the letters of the alphabet down the side of a page. Try and think of adjectives to describe the Alphabet Cat.

The Alphabet Cat

A an *amazing* cat

B a *brave* cat

Don't worry if you can't think of one for every letter!

Practise your punctuation

1. Make up a suitable ending for each sentence.
   a) The lovely princess ...
   b) The old lady ...
   c) One day, a white rabbit ...

2. Check that your sentences make sense. Check that you have used capital letters and full stops correctly.

3. Underline any adjectives in your sentences.

UNIT 10 Prepositions

A **preposition** is a word that tells us
the **position** of one thing in relation to another.

The mouse hid **under** a bush.

The lion was caught **in** a net.

The **prepositions** tell us where the lion and the mouse were.

Practice

Copy these sentences. Underline the preposition in each.

1. The lion is standing by the tree.

2. The mouse is on the chair.

3. The helicopter is above the house.

4. The squirrel jumped off the wall.

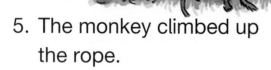

5. The monkey climbed up the rope.

6. The crocodile went into the river.

Making sure

1. Think of a suitable preposition to complete each sentence.

   a) The mouse ran _____ a hole.

   b) The wind blew the man's hat _____ his head.

   c) The silly boy ran _____ the road without looking.

   d) Youssef hid _____ a tree.

   e) The burglar climbed _____ the fence.

   f) The train sped _____ the tunnel.

2. Make up some sentences of your own.
   Use these prepositions in your sentences.

beside	between	below	behind	beneath

Practise your punctuation

1. Arrange these words so that they make sentences.

   a) wood through a walked fox a

   b) up mouse a the clock ran

   c) is money pocket the my in

   d) wall ball Sam over the kicked the

   e) the hidden some rock treasure is under

2. Check that you have used capital letters and full stops correctly.

3. Underline the preposition in each sentence.

Progress Test A

1.

above	in	below

Write a sentence about each picture. Say where the aeroplane is. Use the **prepositions** in the box.

a) The aeroplane is _____ the hangar.

b) The aeroplane is _____ the helicopter.

c) The aeroplane is _____ the clouds.

2. Choose **a** or **an** to fill each gap.
   a) _____ ambulance b) _____ dinosaur c) _____ cake
   d) _____ orange e) _____ red pen f) _____ duck

3. Draw a chart like this in your book.
   Write each of the **nouns** in the box in the correct column.

Things we wear	Things we read	Things we eat

sock	newspaper	cake	eggs	pants	book
comic	jumper	bread	magazine	apple	coat

4. Think of a suitable **noun** to go with each **adjective**.

   a) a tall _____   b) a heavy _____   c) a sharp _____

   d) a red _____   e) a wet _____   f) a dark _____

   g) an ugly _____   h) a yellow _____   i) a sweet _____

5. Write a **sentence** about each picture.
   Circle the **nouns**. Underline the **verbs**.
   The first one has been done for you.

   a) crocodile   b) frog   c) eagle   d) shark   e) koala

   is crawling   is hopping   is flying   is swimming   is climbing

   The (crocodile) is crawling.

6. Copy these **sentences**.
   Write a suitable **verb** in each space.

   Sam _____ off the television. She _____ her mum a
   kiss and _____ the dog. Then Sam _____ upstairs.
   She _____ off her clothes and _____ on her
   nightdress. She _____ her face and _____ her teeth.
   Sam _____ into bed and _____ a book.
   Soon she _____ asleep.

Proper Nouns (1)

A **proper noun** is the name of a **particular person**, **place** or **thing**.

My name is **Duncan**.
I come from **Denmark**.
I go to **Dragon School**.

Notice that **proper nouns** always begin with **capital letters**.

Practice

Here are some names. They should all begin with capital letters. Write them correctly.

1. emma

2. ben

3. mrs patel

4. mr green

5. snow white

6. humpty dumpty

Making sure

1. Copy these sentences, filling the spaces with information about yourself.
   a) My name is _____.
   b) The names of some other members of my family are _____.
   c) I go to _____ School.
   d) My teacher's name is _____.

2. Make up a name for each of these pets.
   a) dog   b) cat
   c) dragon   d) gorilla

3. Write the names of:
   a) five of your friends
   b) five countries in Europe
   c) five of your favourite characters (from television or books)

Practise your punctuation

1. Copy these sentences, putting in the capital letters, full stops and question marks.
   a) can you tell me the way to london
   b) ben and emma come from dover
   c) the capital of wales is cardiff
   d) is edinburgh a big city in scotland
   e) the toy shop was in king street
   f) mount everest is a very high mountain

2. Underline any proper nouns in the sentences you have written.

Proper Nouns (2)

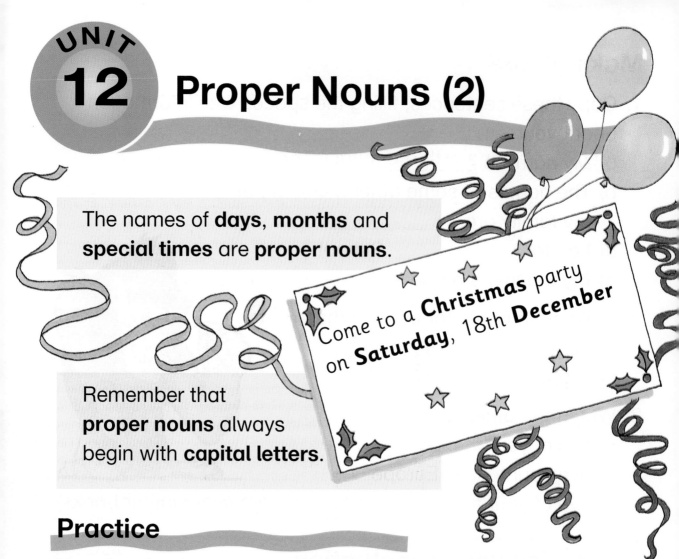

The names of **days**, **months** and **special times** are **proper nouns**.

Come to a **Christmas** party on **Saturday**, 18th **December**

Remember that **proper nouns** always begin with **capital letters**.

Practice

Rewrite the lines of this poem in the correct order.
Begin the name of each day with a capital letter.
Start like this: Monday's child eats fish and chips.

tuesday's child spits apple pips.
thursday's child eats the most.
saturday's child is very rude.
monday's child eats fish and chips.
wednesday's child eats beans on toast.
friday's child is full of food.
But a child who is born on a sunday
has sunshine for dinner every day.

Monday Fish and Chips
Tuesday
Wednesday
Thursday
Friday
Saturday
Sunday

Making sure

1. Here are the names of the months in alphabetical order.
   Write them in the correct order, starting with January.
   Begin each one with a capital letter.

   april   august   december   february   january   july   june
           march   may   november   october   september

2. Read this poem and then answer the questions.

Thirty days hath September,
April, June and November.
All the rest have thirty-one
Except for February alone
And that has twenty-eight days clear
And twenty-nine in each leap year.

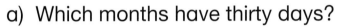

a) Which months have thirty days?
b) Which months have thirty-one days?
c) Which is the shortest month?

Practise your punctuation

Copy these sentences, putting in the capital letters and full stops.

1. christians celebrate christmas in december
2. jews celebrate hanukkah in december too
3. muslims celebrate id in either february or march
4. hindus celebrate diwali in either october or november
5. sikhs celebrate baisakhi in april
6. buddhists celebrate wesak in may or june

Verb Tenses (past and present)

The owl **is flying** through the wood.

Sometimes **verbs** are written in the **present tense**. They tell us what is happening **now**.

Last night the owl **flew** through the wood.

Sometimes **verbs** are written in the **past tense**. They tell us what happened **some time ago**.

Practice

1. Copy these sentences. The verbs are all in the present tense. Underline each verb. The first one has been done for you.

   a) Ben <u>is washing</u> his face. Yesterday Ben washed his face.
   b) Ben is reading a book.
   c) Ben is watching television.
   d) Ben is climbing a tree.
   e) Ben is painting a picture.
   f) Ben is kicking a ball.

2. Now write each sentence again in the past tense. The first one has been done for you.

Making sure

1. Copy this passage about owls. Fill each space with one of the verbs in the box. The verbs are all in the present tense.

hunt	have	sleep	eat	fly

Owls _____ during the day. At night they
_____ through the woods and _____
for food. Owls _____ sharp eyes.
They _____ small animals like mice.

2. Now copy this passage. Fill each space with one of the verbs in the box. The verbs are all in the past tense.

looked	dived	sat	flapped	ran	heard

Olly the owl _____ on the branch of the tree. Slowly
he _____ all around. Suddenly he _____ a
noise. A mouse _____ through the grass below. Olly
_____ his wings and _____ towards the mouse.

Practise your punctuation

1. The words in these sentences have no spaces between them. Write the sentences again, leaving spaces between the words.
a) Theboyjumpedup.   b) YesterdaySamwalkedtoschool.
c) Iameatingmydinner.   d) Somechildrenareshouting.

2. Now underline all the verbs which are in the present tense. Circle all the verbs which are in the past tense.

Using Commas (in lists)

Punctuation marks help us to make **sense** of what we are reading.

. A **full stop** tells us to stop. We have come to the **end of a sentence**.

? A **question mark** tells us that a question is being asked.

, A **comma** tells us to **pause**. It is used to separate items in a list.

Here are the tigers, camels, zebras, giraffes and lions.

In a list we do **not** use a comma before the word **and**.

Practice

Copy these sentences. Put in the missing commas.

1. At the zoo we saw penguins emus ostriches lions and elephants.

2. In my bag I have a book a pencil a ruler an apple and some crisps.

3. Ali had a cat a dog two goldfish a budgie and a gerbil.

4. Ruth has a round face black hair brown eyes a small nose and freckles.

Making sure

1. Write a list of the things which belong to each person.
   The first one has been done for you.

1. footballer   2. astronaut   3. builder   4. hairdresser

A footballer needs a ball, some shorts, a pair of boots and a jersey.

hammer	ball	comb	helmet	shorts	radio	ladder
computer	nails	scissors	mirror	shampoo		
jersey	boots	spacesuit	screwdriver			

2. Complete these sentences.
   List five items in each one.
   a) For my birthday I would like ...
   b) Five sounds I can hear in the street are ...
   c) In the fridge at home we keep ...

Practise your punctuation

Punctuate these sentences correctly. Put in the capital letters, full stops, question marks and commas.

1. jane likes hamburgers pizzas spaghetti and curry
2. where did jason get his hair cut
3. on tuesday lee stayed at home
4. on holiday emma has visited france italy spain greece and holland
5. did you see any zebras at the zoo

Singular and Plural

We can write **nouns** in the **singular** or the **plural**.
Singular means just **one**.
Plural means **more than one**.

one **rabbit**

↑

singular noun

lots of **rabbits**

↑

plural noun

We just add **s** to the end of many singular nouns
to change them into plural nouns.

Practice

Copy and complete this table.

Singular	Plural
farmer	farmers
field	
gate	
	cows
rabbit	
cabbage	

Making sure

watch**es**

dish**es**

glass**es**

fox**es**

1. Some plurals are trickier. We have to add **es** to singular nouns that end in **ch**, **sh**, **ss** or **x**.

   Draw a chart like this in your book. Write each of the singular nouns in the box in the correct column.

ch words	*sh* words	*ss* words	*x* words
match			

fox	match	wish	dash	six	kiss	bunch
	miss	brush	dress	box	catch	

2. Now write the plural of each word. The first one has been done for you.   one match but lots of matches

Practise your punctuation

1. Punctuate these sentences correctly. Put in the capital letters, full stops, question marks and commas.
   a) on the coach there were fifteen girls and twenty boys
   b) mrs green had two trees and five bushes in her garden
   c) tom likes apples oranges pears and peaches
   d) have you seen my pencil and my ruler

2. Now underline all the singular nouns and circle all the plural nouns.

UNIT 16 Opposites (adjectives)

Opposites are words whose meanings are as **different** as possible from each other.

a **good** dog   a **bad** dog

These words are **adjectives**.
They are **opposite** in meaning.

Practice

Copy these lists of adjectives. Join up the opposites in each list. The first one has been done for you.

1.

fat	sad
long	hard
happy	thin
narrow	dry
wet	short
soft	wide

2.

heavy	strong
far	slow
big	near
weak	light
noisy	small
fast	quiet

Making sure

Use adjectives from the 'opposites wheel' below to finish the sentences.

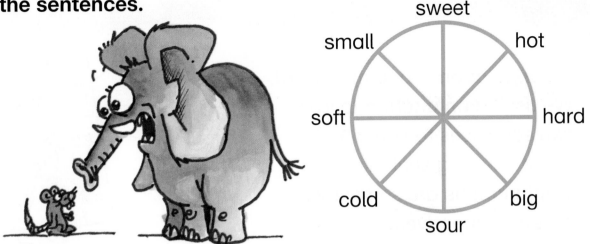

1. A mouse is _____ but an elephant is _____.
2. A rock is _____ but cotton wool is _____.
3. Ice is _____ but the sun is _____.
4. A lemon is _____ but sugar is _____.

Practise your punctuation

1. Punctuate these sentences correctly.
   Put in the capital letters, full stops and question marks.
   a) dan drew a straight line   b) do you like sweet things
   c) ruth's skirt was dirty   d) is my dinner hot
   e) the sea was calm   f) are zebras wild animals

2. Now underline the adjective in each sentence.
   Write each sentence again. Replace each adjective
   with a word opposite in meaning.

Conjunctions

A **conjunction** is a **joining** word. We use a **conjunction** to join two sentences together to make one long sentence. **Conjunctions** are sometimes called **connectives**.

My Gran wrote to me.   +   She told me about her new house.

My Gran wrote to me **and** told me about her new house.

The two sentences have been joined with **and**. This is a **conjunction**.

Practice

Write these pairs of sentences again.
Join each pair of sentences with the conjunction and.
The first one has been done for you.

1. I went to the shop.   I bought a comic.
   I went to the shop and bought a comic.
2. Tom put on his coat.   He went out to play.
3. The dog ran after the cat.   It barked loudly.
4. Megan has curly hair.   She has brown eyes.
5. Ali picked up the kettle.   He filled it with water.

Making sure

Gran is old. + Leanne is young.

Gran is old **but** Leanne is young.

Sometimes we join sentences with the conjunction but.
We use the conjuction but because old is the opposite
of young.

Write these pairs of sentences again.
Join each pair of sentences with the conjunction but.
The first one has been done for you.

1. The red door is shut.   The green door is open.
   The red door is shut but the green door is open.
2. The lorry was slow.   The racing car was fast.
3. Sara's jeans were cheap.   Shireen's jeans were expensive.
4. Mr Naik's bag was heavy.   Mrs Naik's bag was light.
5. Dean is good at maths.   Dean is not good at spelling.

Practise your punctuation

1. Make up a suitable ending for each sentence.
   Remember to punctuate each sentence correctly.
   a) Kate loves pizzas but ...
   b) Nadeem got out of bed and ...
   c) My dog saw a cat in the garden and ...
   d) Frogs hop but ...
   e) Shireen decided to walk to the shop but ...
   f) The postman walked up the path and ...

2. Now underline the conjunction in each sentence.

UNIT 18 Verbs (the verb to be)

The verb **to be** is the most common verb in the English language.

Present tense	Past tense
is	was
are	were

We can use it **on its own**.

This dog **is** a Yorkshire Terrier.

We can use it **as part of another verb**.

The dogs **are eating**.

We use **is** or **was** when we are talking about **one** thing or person.

The dog **was** asleep.

We use **are** or **were** when we are talking about **more than one** thing or person.

The dogs **were** barking.

Practice

Choose the correct form of the verb to be to complete each sentence.

1. The cat (is/are) asleep.
2. The apples (is/are) red.
3. The children (is/are) going to school.
4. The horses (was/were) galloping.
5. The dog (was/were) very small.

Making sure

Choose the correct form of the noun to complete each sentence.

1. The (cake/cakes) is very small.
2. Some (apple/apples) were red.
3. The (spade/spades) was broken.
4. Baby (dog/dogs) are called puppies.
5. The (boy/boys) was reading a comic.
6. The (girl/girls) were listening to the teacher.
7. The (doctor/doctors) is sitting in her office.
8. The (kitten/kittens) are playing with the wool.

Practise your punctuation

Correct the verb in each sentence.
Put in the missing capital letters and full stops.

1. katie and harry was paddling in the water
2. two children was climbing on the roof of the shed
3. the rain are pouring down
4. the men is getting very wet
5. mrs jones were waving to her friend
6. the thief are getting away

UNIT 19   Revision – Adjectives, Nouns, Verbs

An **adjective** is a **describing** word. It tells us more about a **noun**.

A **noun** is a **naming** word. It can be the **name** of a **person**, **place** or **thing**.

A **verb** is a **doing** word. Every **sentence** must have a **verb**.

A **toad catches small insects**.

↑   ↑   ↑   ↑

noun   verb   adjective   noun

Practice

1. Choose the correct noun to complete each sentence.
   a) A (frog/snake) hops.
   b) A (bird/cow) moos.
   c) A (frog/snake) hisses.
   d) A (bird/cow) flies.

2. Choose the correct verb to complete each sentence.
   a) A snail (slides/swings).
   b) Kangaroos (swim/jump).
   c) A fish (is snoring/ is swimming).
   d) Some dogs (were barking/were driving).

3. Choose the correct adjective to complete each sentence.
   a) I had a (far/cold) drink.
   b) My suitcase was very (heavy/prickly).
   c) The lemon tasted (full/sour).
   d) It was a (red/windy) night.

Making sure

1. Copy the sentences. Circle the nouns. Underline the verbs.
   Cross out the adjectives.
   a) The red car sped up the hill. b) Tom felt frightened.
   c) Kim wore a large hat.   d) The bike had a flat tyre.

2. Make up four silly sentences.
   Choose a word from each column for each sentence.
   The first one has been done for you.

Adjective	Noun	Verb	Adjective	Noun
red	children	eat	frozen	fish
heavy	sharks	marry	frightened	teachers
tall	elephants	ride	wobbly	teeth
steaming	astronauts	chase	exploding	oranges

Steaming elephants marry wobbly fish.

Practise your punctuation

1. Think of a silly ending or beginning for each sentence.
   Remember to punctuate your sentences correctly.
   a) Some sizzling sausages ... b) The old door ...
   c) ... in the crowded room.   d) The purple monsters ...
   e) ... through the dark forest.

2. Circle the nouns, underline the verbs and cross out the
   adjectives in your sentences.

Grammar and Punctuation

Grammar is the study of the way in which we make sentences. It looks at how words work together. It is to do with the **rules** of language.

Punctuation helps us to make **sense** of what we read.

Punctuation marks make writing easier for us to understand. They help us to read with **expression**.

slugsslidethroughthelonggrasstheyaresoftandslimy

If we put in **spaces** and **punctuation marks** the writing is much easier to read.

Slugs slide through the long grass. They are soft and slimy.

Practice

Here are some facts about a hedgehog.

- covered with prickly spines
- comes out at night
- makes nest of leaves and grass
- grows up to 25cm long
- sleeps during winter
- curls into ball when attacked

Write six sentences about a hedgehog.
Remember to put in the capital letters and full stops.
Underline the verbs in the sentences you have written.

Making sure

1. Arrange these words so that they make sentences.
   Punctuate the sentences correctly. Underline the verbs.
   a) wanted some home aliens new a
   b) aliens built rocket the a huge
   c) ready got they long for a journey
   d) space off the blasted rocket into
   e) landed it crash when wrong went something a with

2. This alien does not speak in sentences.
   Put his words into sentences, adding any missing words
   and punctuation marks.

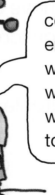

come ... long ... way ... rocket
engine ... not ... work
why ... you ... frightened
want ... be ... friend
where ... live
take ... home ... meet ... family

Practise your punctuation

**Copy this description of the alien.
Punctuate it correctly.**

the alien had a big round body it had a square head
its three green eyes flashed on and off its teeth were
sharp and pointed the alien spoke in a deep voice
with a booming sound it bounced along on a huge
spring which had a large hairy foot at the end of it

Progress Test B

I have four legs and a tail.
People ride on me. I neigh.
What am I?

1. Answer each riddle with a suitable **noun**.
   a) I live on a farm. I give milk. What am I?
   b) I am made of wood. I have a handle. What am I?
   c) I am made of glass. You look in me to see yourself.
      What am I?

2. Fill each space with a suitable **adjective**.
   a) Ice is _____ .   b) A wheel is _____ .
   c) A needle is _____ .   d) The lions were _____ .
   e) A giant is _____ .   f) The teacher was _____ .

3. Copy these sentences.
   Choose **is** or **are** to complete each one.
   a) Puppies _____ cute.   b) Baby cows _____
                                   called calves.
   c) Some children _____   d) The chicken _____
      shouting.   clucking.

4. Now complete each of these sentences with **was** or **were**.
   a) The bus _____ late.   b) The boys _____ scared.
   c) Some cows _____   d) The cat _____ sitting
      mooing.   by the fire.

5. Copy and complete this chart:

Singular	Plural
fox	
	cups
	stitches
jumper	
wish	
	pencils
boss	
	birds
	boxes
hutch	

6. Write the **opposites** of these **nouns**.

   a) day   b) boy   c) summer   d) question   e) friend

7. Write the **opposites** of these **verbs**.

   a) close   b) run   c) stop   d) float   e) whisper

8. Write the **opposites** of these **adjectives**.

   a) high   b) cold   c) hard   d) rough   e) near

9. Join each pair of sentences with a conjunction (**and** or **but**).

   a) I ate a sandwich. Then I drank a cup of tea.

   b) Tom is right. Dan is wrong.

   c) Amy lost. Yasmin won.

   d) Mrs Shah opened the door. She walked in the room.

10. Copy these sentences. Underline the **verbs**.
    a) Emma is playing hopscotch. b) The clouds are grey.
    c) The children are shopping.   d) Every window is broken.
    e) I am painting a picture.   f) We are eating some crisps.

11. Now write each sentence in the **past tense**.

12. Rewrite these sentences correctly. Begin each **proper noun** with a capital letter.
    a) Next tuesday it will be tom's birthday.
    b) christmas is always in december.
    c) Does the river thames flow through london?
    d) france, italy, spain and austria are all countries in europe.

13. Match these beginnings and endings of sentences. Write each sentence correctly.

    a) A sentence is   a joining word.

    b) A verb is   a naming word.

    c) A noun is   a group of words that makes sense on its own.

    d) An adjective is   a word that tells you the position of one thing in relation to another.

    e) A preposition is   a doing word.

    f) A conjunction is   a describing word.